D1274530

SUPERHEROES ON A MEDICAL MISSION
WHAT'S UP WITH ELLA?"
MEDIKIDZ EXPLAIN DIABETES

ENERGY SHACK

rosen publishing's
rosen central
New York

Dr. Kim Chilman-Blair and John Taddeo
Medical content reviewed for accuracy by
Professor Peter Hindmarsh and Professor John Gregory

This edition published in 2010 by:

The Rosen Publishing Group, Inc.
29 East 21st Street
New York, NY 10010

Additional end matter copyright © 2010 by The Rosen Publishing Group, Inc.

Library of Congress Cataloging-in-Publication Data

Chilman-Blair, Kim.
"What's up with Ella?": medikidz explain diabetes / Dr. Kim Chilman-Blair and John Taddeo; medical content reviewed for accuracy by Peter Hindmarsh and John Gregory.
    p. cm. — (Superheroes on a medical mission)
Includes index.
ISBN 978-1-4358-3538-2 (lib. bdg.)
1. Diabetes in children—Comic books, strips, etc. I. Taddeo, John. II. Title.
RJ420.D5C48 2010
618.92'462—dc22

                                                                      2009031612

Manufactured in China

CPSIA Compliance Information: Batch # MW0102YA: For Further Information contact Rosen Publishing, New York, New York at 1-800-237-9932

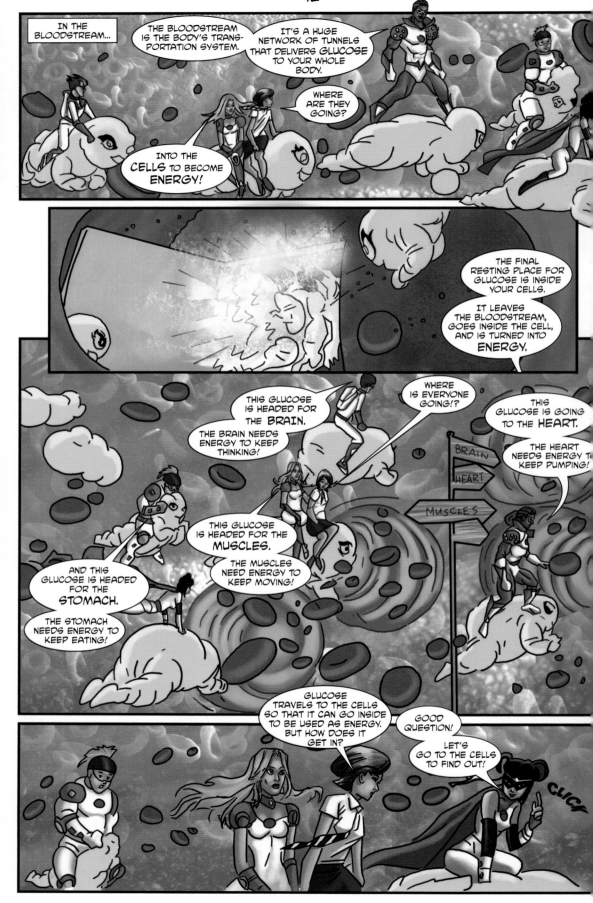

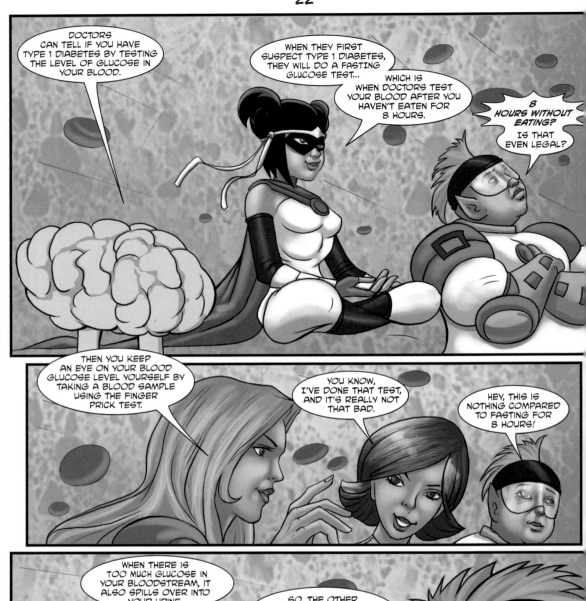

DOCTORS CAN TELL IF YOU HAVE TYPE 1 DIABETES BY TESTING THE LEVEL OF GLUCOSE IN YOUR BLOOD.

WHEN THEY FIRST SUSPECT TYPE 1 DIABETES, THEY WILL DO A FASTING GLUCOSE TEST...

WHICH IS WHEN DOCTORS TEST YOUR BLOOD AFTER YOU HAVEN'T EATEN FOR 8 HOURS.

8 HOURS WITHOUT EATING? IS THAT EVEN LEGAL?

THEN YOU KEEP AN EYE ON YOUR BLOOD GLUCOSE LEVEL YOURSELF BY TAKING A BLOOD SAMPLE USING THE FINGER PRICK TEST.

YOU KNOW, I'VE DONE THAT TEST, AND IT'S REALLY NOT THAT BAD.

HEY, THIS IS NOTHING COMPARED TO FASTING FOR 8 HOURS!

WHEN THERE IS TOO MUCH GLUCOSE IN YOUR BLOODSTREAM, IT ALSO SPILLS OVER INTO YOUR URINE.

SO, THE OTHER WAY TO TEST FOR DIABETES IS TO CHECK THE GLUCOSE LEVEL IN YOUR URINE!

LIKE IN THIS SAMPLE I PREPARED EARLIER!

THAT'S REALLY GROSS.

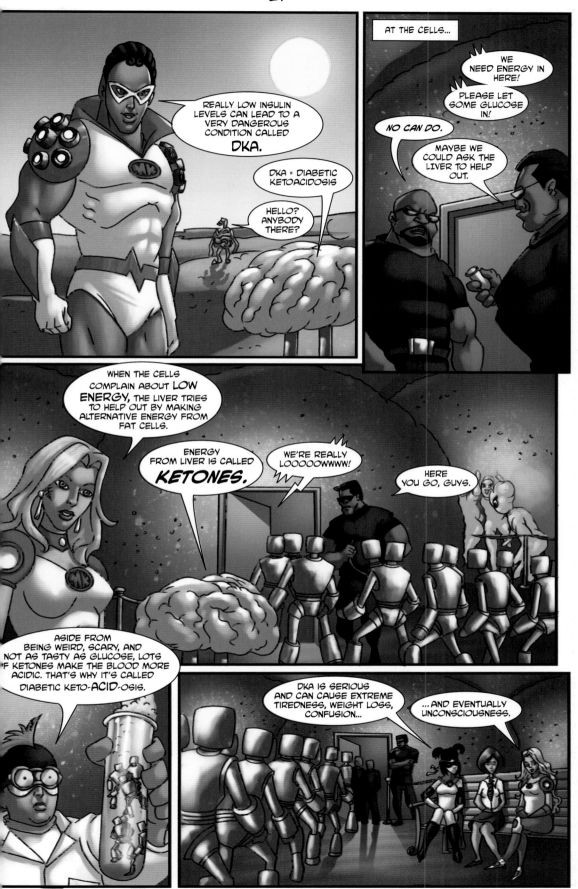

THEY'RE BACK! AXON IS BACK!

DID YOU SEE ANY COOL ROBOTS?

I LEARNED ALL ABOUT MY TYPE 1 DIABETES!

AND I OWE IT ALL TO...

AXON!

AXON!

AXON!

AXON!

HOLD IT! HOLD IT! JUST A SECOND, PLEASE. JUST A MOMENT, PLEASE! ATTENTION, PLEASE.

PLEASE DON'T INTERRUPT THEM WHILE THEY ARE ADORING ME.

THANK YOU.

QUIET!

WE HAVE TIME FOR A FEW QUESTIONS, AND THEN WE HAVE TO GO.

YES, YOU?

WHAT'S IT LIKE TO KNOW AXON?

NEXT QUESTION, PLEASE.

NEXT QUESTION, PLEASE.

HOW GREAT IS IT TO HAVE AXON AS YOUR FRIEND?

HOW HAS AXON INSPIRED YOU IN YOUR ROBOTIC CONSTRUCTION ENDEAVORS?

GUYS, DOES ANYONE HAVE ANY QUESTIONS ABOUT TYPE 1 DIABETES?

WHAT'S IT LIKE TO TEACH KIDS ABOUT TYPE 1 DIABETES WITH AXON?

THAT'S IT, WE'RE OUT OF HERE. THOSE KIDS ARE CLEARLY CRAZY!

NO, YOU CAN'T TAKE ME FROM MY PEOPLE.

AXON!

AXON!

AXON!

AXON, SIT DOWN!

GLOSSARY

BETA CELL A TYPE OF CELL IN THE PANCREAS THAT MAKES AND RELEASES INSULIN, WHICH CONTROLS THE LEVEL OF GLUCOSE IN THE BLOOD.

BLOOD VESSELS HOLLOW TUBES THAT CIRCULATE BLOOD THROUGHOUT THE BODY.

BRAIN THE CENTER OF THE HUMAN NERVOUS SYSTEM, CONTROLLING THOUGHT, INVOLUNTARY MOVEMENT IN THE BODY, BALANCE, GROWTH, AND TEMPERATURE CONTROL.

DIABETIC KETOACIDOSIS (DKA) A POTENTIALLY LIFE-THREATENING COMPLICATION OF DIABETES CAUSED BY A SHORTAGE OF INSULIN IN THE BODY. IN RESPONSE TO THE SHORTAGE, GLUCOSE CANNOT ENTER THE CELLS FOR ENERGY, AND THE BODY SWITCHES TO BURNING FAT INSTEAD. THIS PRODUCES TOXIC ACIDS KNOWN AS KETONES.

ENERGY AN ENTITY OF NATURE WHERE LEVELS OF FUEL MAKE IT POSSIBLE FOR A BODY TO FUNCTION.

FINGER PRICK TEST A TEST USED TO MONITOR GLUCOSE LEVELS IN THE BLOOD. THE FINGER IS PRICKED TO OBTAIN A DROP OF BLOOD AND THEN TESTED USING A BLOOD GLUCOSE MONITOR.

GLUCOSE A SIMPLE SUGAR AND ONE OF THE MAIN ENERGY SOURCES IN THE HUMAN BODY.

HEART THE MUSCULAR ORGAN OF THE CIRCULATORY SYSTEM THAT IS RESPONSIBLE FOR PUMPING BLOOD THROUGHOUT THE BODY.

HEART ATTACK WHEN BLOOD FLOW TO A SECTION OF HEART MUSCLE BECOMES BLOCKED. IF THE FLOW OF BLOOD ISN'T RESTORED QUICKLY, THE SECTION OF HEART MUSCLE BECOMES DAMAGED FROM LACK OF OXYGEN AND BEGINS TO DIE.

HYPERGLYCEMIA A CONDITION IN WHICH AN EXCESSIVE AMOUNT OF GLUCOSE CIRCULATES IN THE BLOOD.

HYPOGLYCEMIA A CONDITION CHARACTERIZED BY AN ABNORMALLY LOW LEVEL OF GLUCOSE IN THE BLOOD.

IMMUNE SYSTEM A GROUP OF SPECIAL CELLS, PROTEINS, TISSUES, AND ORGANS THAT SEEK OUT AND DESTROY ORGANISMS OR SUBSTANCES THAT CAUSE DISEASE.

INSULIN A PROTEIN THAT IS ESSENTIAL FOR THE METABOLISM OF CARBOHYDRATES AND REGULATION OF GLUCOSE LEVELS IN THE BLOOD.

INTESTINE THE PART OF THE DIGESTIVE TRACT WHERE NUTRIENTS ARE ABSORBED BY THE BODY.

KETONES COMPOUNDS THAT ARE PRODUCED AS BY-PRODUCTS WHEN FATTY ACIDS ARE BROKEN DOWN FOR ENERGY IN THE LIVER AND KIDNEY.

LIVER THE LARGEST ORGAN INSIDE OF YOUR BODY. IT HELPS TURN FOOD INTO ENERGY, CLEANS ALCOHOL AND POISONS FROM THE BLOOD, AND MAKES BILE, A LIQUID THAT HELPS WITH DIGESTION.

MUSCLE ELASTIC TISSUE THAT CONTRACTS TO ENABLE MOVEMENT WITHIN THE BODY.

PANCREAS ORGAN BEHIND THE LIVER WHERE INSULIN IS PRODUCED.

STOMACH THE ORGAN IN THE DIGESTIVE SYSTEM WHERE THE BULK OF DIGESTION OCCURS.

STROKE MEDICAL CONDITION WHERE BLOOD FLOW TO THE BRAIN STOPS BECAUSE OF CLOTTING OR BREAKAGE IN THE BLOOD VESSELS.

VIRUS A MICROSCOPIC INFECTIOUS AGENT THAT CAN REPRODUCE ONLY INSIDE A HOST CELL.

FOR MORE INFORMATION

AMERICAN DIABETES ASSOCIATION
1701 NORTH BEAUREGARD STREET
ALEXANDRIA, VA 22311
(800) 342-2383
WEB SITE: HTTP://WWW.DIABETES.ORG
AN ASSOCIATION THAT FUNDS RESEARCH TO PREVENT, CURE, AND
    MANAGE DIABETES; PROVIDES SERVICES TO COMMUNITIES;
    PROVIDES INFORMATION ABOUT THE DISEASE; AND PROTECTS
    HUMAN RIGHTS.

AMERICAN LIVER FOUNDATION
75 MAIDEN LANE, SUITE 603
NEW YORK, NY 10038
(212) 668-1000
WEB SITE: HTTP://WWW.LIVERFOUNDATION.ORG
THE FOUNDATION FACILITATES, ADVOCATES, AND PROMOTES
    EDUCATION, SUPPORT, AND RESEARCH FOR THE PREVENTION,
    TREATMENT, AND CURE OF LIVER DISEASE.

AMERICAN PANCREATIC ASSOCIATION
P.O. BOX 14906
MINNEAPOLIS, MN 55414
(612) 626-9797
WEB SITE: HTTP://WWW.AMERICAN-PANCREATIC-ASSOCIATION.ORG
THIS ORGANIZATION IS DEVOTED TO PROMOTING UNDERSTAND-
    ING OF THE PANCREAS, ITS NATURAL FUNCTIONS, AND
    DISORDERS.

NATIONAL DIABETES EDUCATION PROGRAM
1 DIABETES WAY
BETHESDA, MD 20814
(800) 438-9692
WEB SITE: HTTP://WWW.NDEP.NIH.GOV
THE PROGRAM KEEPS THE PUBLIC INFORMED ABOUT
    CONTROLLING TYPE 1 DIABETES AND AVOIDING TYPE 2
    DIABETES.

**NATIONAL INSTITUTE OF DIABETES AND DIGESTIVE AND
    KIDNEY DISEASES**
NIH BUILDING 31, ROOM 9A06
31 CENTER DRIVE, MSC 2560
BETHESDA, MD 20892
(301) 496-3583
WEB SITE: HTTP://WWW2.NIDDK.NIH.GOV

THIS NATIONAL INSTITUTE CONDUCTS AND SUPPORTS BASIC AND
   CLINICAL RESEARCH ON MANY SERIOUS DISEASES AFFECTING
   PUBLIC HEALTH.

NATIONAL LIBRARY OF MEDICINE
8600 ROCKVILLE PIKE
BETHESDA, MD 20894
(888) 346-3656
WEB SITE: HTTP://WWW.NLM.NIH.GOV
THIS IS THE WORLD'S LARGEST MEDICAL LIBRARY.

PUBLIC HEALTH AGENCY OF CANADA
130 COLONNADE ROAD
A.L. 6501H
OTTAWA, ON K1A OK9
CANADA
WEB SITE: HTTP://WWW.PUBLICHEALTH.GC.CA
THE AGENCY IS DEDICATED TO PROTECTING AND IMPROVING THE
   HEALTH OF CANADIANS.

WEB SITES

DUE TO THE CHANGING NATURE OF INTERNET LINKS, ROSEN
PUBLISHING HAS DEVELOPED AN ONLINE LIST OF WEB SITES
RELATED TO THE SUBJECT OF THIS BOOK. THIS SITE IS UPDATED
REGULARLY. PLEASE USE THIS LINK TO ACCESS THE LIST:

HTTP://WWW.ROSENLINKS.COM/MED/DIAB

FOR FURTHER READING

AMERICAN DIABETES ASSOCIATION COMPLETE GUIDE TO DIABETES. NEW YORK, NY: BANTAM, 2006.

BERNSTEIN, RICHARD K. *DR. BERNSTEIN'S DIABETES SOLUTION: THE COMPLETE GUIDE TO ACHIEVING NORMAL BLOOD SUGARS.* NEW YORK, NY: LITTLE, BROWN, 2007.

BLISS, MICHAEL. *THE DISCOVERY OF INSULIN.* CHICAGO, IL: UNIVERSITY OF CHICAGO PRESS, 2007.

COLBERG, SHERI R. *DIABETIC ATHLETE'S HANDBOOK.* CHAMPAIGN, IL: HUMAN KINETICS PUBLISHERS, 2008.

COLBERG, SHERI R., AND STEVEN V. EDELMAN. *50 SECRETS OF THE LONGEST LIVING PEOPLE WITH DIABETES.* CAMBRIDGE, MA: DA CAPO PRESS, 2007.

CONKLING, WINIFRED, AND DEBORAH MITCHELL. *LIVING WELL WITH DIABETES.* NEW YORK, NY: ST. MARTIN'S, 2009.

FOX, CHARLES, AND ANNE KILVERT. *TYPE 1 DIABETES: ANSWERS AT YOUR FINGERTIPS.* 6TH ED. LONDON, ENGLAND: CLASS PUBLISHING, 2007.

HANAS, RAGNAR, M.D. *TYPE 1 DIABETES: A GUIDE FOR CHILDREN, ADOLESCENTS, YOUNG ADULTS–AND THEIR CAREGIVERS.* CAMBRIDGE, MA: DA CAPO PRESS, 2005.

MASHARANI, UMESH. *DIABETES DEMYSTIFIED: A SELF-TEACHING GUIDE.* NEW YORK, NY: MCGRAW-HILL, 2007.

MAYO CLINIC: THE ESSENTIAL DIABETES BOOK. NEW YORK, NY: TIME, 2009.

REDDY, SETHU. *THE CLEVELAND CLINIC GUIDE TO DIABETES.* NEW YORK, NY: KAPLAN, 2009.

RUBIN, ALAN L., M.D. *TYPE 1 DIABETES FOR DUMMIES.* HOBOKEN, NJ: WILEY, 2008.

SCHEINER, GARY, M.S. *THINK LIKE A PANCREAS: A PRACTICAL GUIDE TO MANAGING DIABETES WITH INSULIN.* CAMBRIDGE, MA: DA CAPO PRESS, 2004.

SMITH, TOM. *LIVING WITH TYPE 1 DIABETES.* LONDON, ENGLAND: SHELDON PRESS, 2009.

TEENAGERS WITH TYPE 1 DIABETES : A CURRICULUM FOR ADOLESCENTS AND FAMILIES. ALEXANDRIA, VA: AMERICAN DIABETES ASSOCIATION, 2003.

WEISS, MICHAEL A., AND MARTHA MITCHELL FUNNELL. *THE LITTLE DIABETES BOOK YOU NEED TO READ.* PHILADELPHIA, PA: RUNNING PRESS, 2007.

YU, WINNIE, MELVIN R. STJERNHOLM, AND ALEXIS MUNIER. *WHAT TO DO WHEN THE DOCTOR SAYS IT'S DIABETES: THE MOST IMPORTANT THINGS YOU NEED TO KNOW ABOUT BLOOD SUGAR, DIET, AND EXERCISE FOR TYPE I AND TYPE II DIABETES.* BEVERLY, MA: FAIR WINDS PRESS, 2004.

INDEX

A
APPENDIX, 18

B
BERRY, HALLE, 31
BETA CELLS, 14-16, 18
BLOOD VESSELS, 26
BRAIN, 4, 6, 12, 19, 24, 26

D
DIABETES
    CELEBRITIES WITH, 31
    COMPLICATIONS FROM, 25-27
    CURE FOR, 31
    DIAGNOSING, 22-23, 25
    MANAGING, 4-5, 9, 26, 28-31
    SYMPTOMS OF, 24-25
DIABETIC KETOACIDOSIS
    (DKA), 27

F
FINGER PRICK TEST, 22

G
GLUCOSE, 4, 9, 10-14, 19-22,
    24-31

H
HEART, 7, 12, 19, 26
HEART ATTACK, 26
HYPERGLYCEMIA, 21
HYPOGLYCEMIA, 29

I
IMMUNE SYSTEM, 16-17
INSULIN, 5, 9, 13-15, 18-20, 27-31
INTESTINE, 11

K
KETONES, 27
KIDNEYS, 26

L
LIVER, 27
LUNGS, 6, 7

M
MUSCLES, 12

P
PANCREAS, 9, 13-15, 18, 26, 28

S
STOMACH, 10, 12-13, 15, 18
STROKE, 26

T
TYPE II DIABETES, 21

U
URINE, 22, 25

V
VIRUS, 16-17

W
WHITE BLOOD CELLS, 17

ABOUT THE AUTHORS

DR. KIM CHILMAN-BLAIR IS A MEDICAL DOCTOR WITH TEN YEARS' EXPERIENCE OF MEDICAL WRITING, AND A PASSION FOR PROVIDING MEDICAL INFORMATION THAT MAKES CHILDREN WANT TO LEARN.

JOHN TADDEO, FORMALLY OF MARVEL ENTERTAINMENT, IS A CELEBRATED COMIC BOOK WRITER AND DIRECTOR OF TWO AWARD-WINNING ANIMATED-SHORTS.